P9-DVC-597

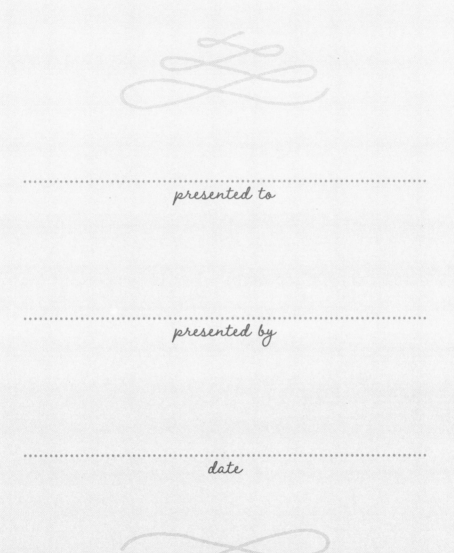

....

presented to

....

presented by

....

date

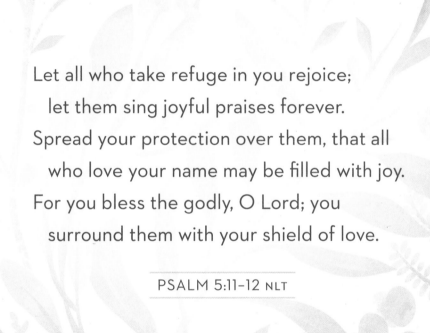

Let all who take refuge in you rejoice;
　　let them sing joyful praises forever.
Spread your protection over them, that all
　　who love your name may be filled with joy.
For you bless the godly, O Lord; you
　　surround them with your shield of love.

PSALM 5:11–12 NLT

Blessings for the Soul

Words of Grace and Peace for Your Heart

SUSIE LARSON

BETHANYHOUSE

a division of Baker Publishing Group
Minneapolis, Minnesota

© 2016 by Susie Larson

Published by Bethany House Publishers
11400 Hampshire Avenue South
Bloomington, Minnesota 55438
www.bethanyhouse.com

Bethany House Publishers is a division of
Baker Publishing Group, Grand Rapids, Michigan

Previously published under the title *Blessings for Women*.

Printed in China

All rights reserved. No part of this publication may be reproduced, stored in a retrieval system, or transmitted in any form or by any means—for example, electronic, photocopy, recording—without the prior written permission of the publisher. The only exception is brief quotations in printed reviews.

Library of Congress Control Number: 2016938460

ISBN: 978-0-7642-3451-4

Unless otherwise indicated, Scripture quotations are from the Holy Bible, New International Version®. NIV®. Copyright © 1973, 1978, 1984, 2011 by Biblica, Inc.™ Used by permission of Zondervan. All rights reserved worldwide. www.zondervan.com

Scripture quotations labeled THE MESSAGE are from *The Message* by Eugene H. Peterson, copyright © 1993, 1994, 1995, 2000, 2001, 2002. Used by permission of NavPress. All rights reserved. Represented by Tyndale House Publishers, Inc.

Scripture quotations labeled NKJV are from the New King James Version®. Copyright © 1982 by Thomas Nelson, Inc. Used by permission. All rights reserved.

Scripture quotations labeled NLT are from the Holy Bible, New Living Translation, copyright © 1996, 2004, 2015 by Tyndale House Foundation. Used by permission of Tyndale House Publishers, Inc., Carol Stream, Illinois 60188. All rights reserved.

Scripture quotations labeled TLB are from The Living Bible, copyright © 1971. Used by permission of Tyndale House Publishers, Inc., Carol Stream, Illinois 60188. All rights reserved.

Scripture quotations labeled THE VOICE are from The Voice Bible, copyright © 2012 Thomas Nelson, Inc. The Voice™ translation © 2012 Ecclesia Bible Society. All rights reserved.

Cover design by Emily Weigel
Interior design by William Overbeeke
Interior and cover floral art by Ira Khroniuk

Author is represented by The Steve Laube Agency

19   20   21   22   23   24   25   7   6   5   4   3   2   1

To Jesus,
who's always up to
something new

Contents

To You, My Friend

God loves you with an everlasting love. He is faithful, wise, and true. He is a miracle-working, soul-saving, life-transforming God, and He cares deeply about you.

As you work your way through these pages, may you grow to know—on a much deeper level—what you possess when you have Christ. He is above all, in all, and through all. He is the way, the truth, and the life. He promises never to leave you, never to forsake you, and never to let go of your hand. Life on earth is hard sometimes, but life with God is always good, always beautiful, and forever eternal. The Lord wants you to last long and finish strong, and He's the one who will keep you strong to the end.

May these blessings be yours in every way.

—Susie Larson

Also, please don't miss the blessings near the end of the book for specific needs and occasions: A Life-Giving Weekend, For Restored Health, Christmas, A New Year, Father's Day, and Declaration of Dependence.

Blessings
for the Soul

The Lord is my shepherd, I lack nothing. He makes me lie down in green pastures, he leads me beside quiet waters, he refreshes my soul. He guides me along the right paths for his name's sake.

PSALM 23:1–3

Rest Awhile

May Jesus lead you beside still waters and restore your soul.

May time in His presence stir up fresh faith in you.

May the power of His Word reignite your prayers.

May the wonder of His love overwhelm you and fill you up again. And may His perfect promises remind you that you're never alone, never without help, and always near to His heart.

Raise your arms, open your hands, and receive all God has for you this day!

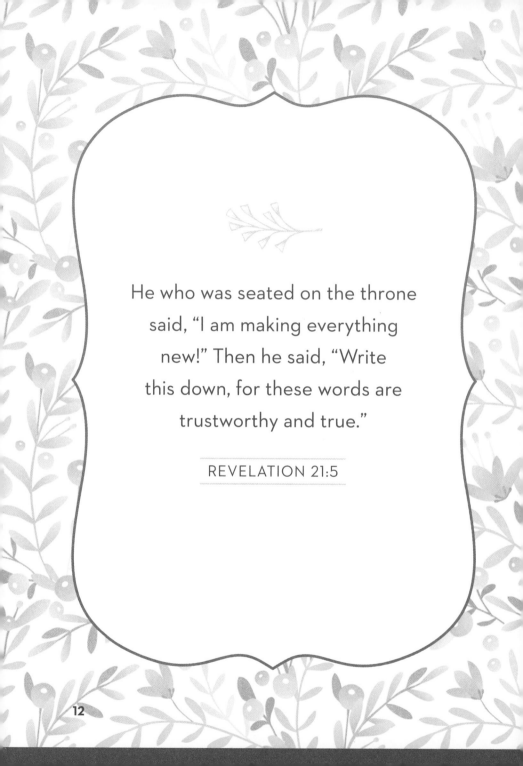

He who was seated on the throne
said, "I am making everything
new!" Then he said, "Write
this down, for these words are
trustworthy and true."

REVELATION 21:5

God Is Moving

May you dare to believe that God is moving in your life, because He is. He makes all things new. And He intends to dismantle the schemes of the enemy. Will you trust Him?

May your next steps be faith steps and your next words, faith words.

May you embrace a joyful heart, not because of what your eyes see, but because of what your heart knows: God is good, He is for you, and He WILL NOT fail you.

Have a blessed day.

Do not be anxious about anything, but in every situation, by prayer and petition, with thanksgiving, present your requests to God. And the peace of God, which transcends all understanding, will guard your hearts and your minds in Christ Jesus.

PHILIPPIANS 4:6-7

Trust Him Fully

May you entrust your whole soul and story to the God who saves, loves, and establishes you.

Jesus, your precious Shepherd, leads you even when you're unaware. The more you trust Him, the more you'll enjoy the peace that passes understanding and defies your circumstances.

Read His Word. Listen for His voice. Do what He says. Enjoy the journey. He'll get you where you need to go.

Walk with me and work with me—watch how I do it. Learn the unforced rhythms of grace. I won't lay anything heavy or ill-fitting on you. Keep company with me and you'll learn to live freely and lightly.

MATTHEW 11:29–30 THE MESSAGE

Grace for Today

May you pause right now and give your burdens to Jesus. He'll carry what's too heavy for you. He'll give you grace to carry His assignment for you.

May you release the worries that slow you down and make life unnecessarily burdensome.

May you choose the discipline of joy and discover a new strength in the process.

You are loved, called, cherished, anointed, and appointed. Refuse yesterday's baggage, today's insecurities, or tomorrow's worries.

You've got Jesus and He's got you.

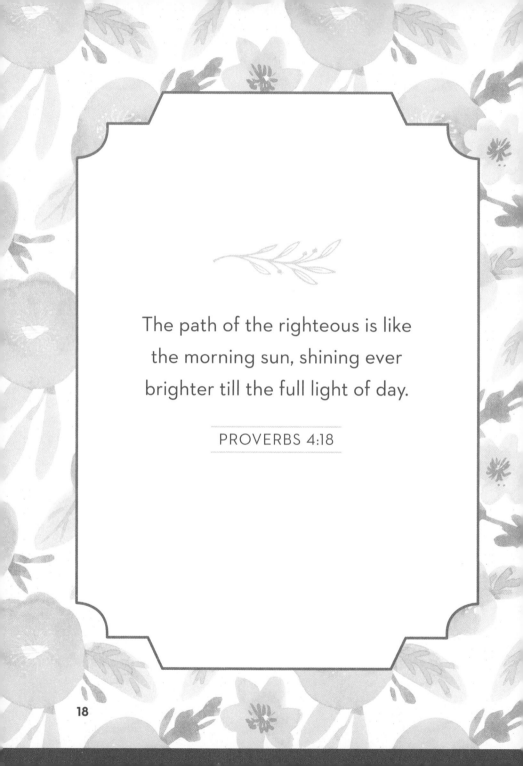

The path of the righteous is like the morning sun, shining ever brighter till the full light of day.

PROVERBS 4:18

Spiritual Momentum

May God wildly increase your capacity to walk with Him.

May His power and His promises impact your every word and every step. May He increase your territory, establish your influence, and awaken your faith.

May He deepen your love, broaden your perspective, and multiply your compassion.

In every way, may you know God's redeeming, multiplying power in your life. And may humble and holy spiritual momentum be yours.

Walk forward in faith today.

The Lord your God is with you,
the Mighty Warrior who saves. He
will take great delight in you; in his
love he will no longer rebuke you, but
will rejoice over you with singing.

ZEPHANIAH 3:17

God's Powerful Love

May God fine-tune your spiritual ears so you hear heaven's song above the chaos and the noise.

May you rest in the knowledge that God is in control and will have the last say when it's all said and done.

Though the elements rage and the enemy taunts, God is the one who fights for you and He will win for you. He loves you with power and with passion.

May His kingdom come and His will be done everywhere you place your feet today.

Have a powerful day in Him!

When she speaks, her words
are wise, and she gives
instructions with kindness.

PROVERBS 31:26 NLT

Your Influence Matters

In the days ahead, may you die to the power of others' opinions and instead live out of the relentless, abundant love God has for you.

As people become more cruel and careless with their opinions, may you become more loving and discerning with yours.

May you speak with precision, pray with power, and stand in courage. Your life and influence matter deeply in this desperate world.

Lean in and learn everything you can from the One who loves you deeply and intends to use you greatly.

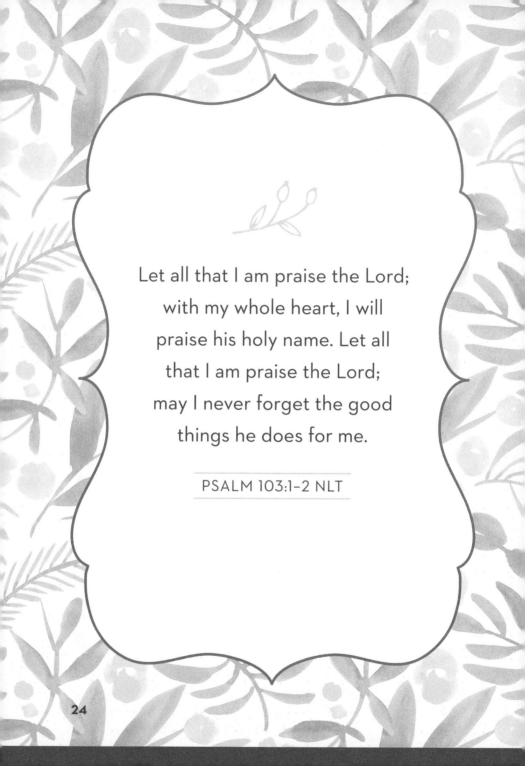

Let all that I am praise the Lord;
with my whole heart, I will
praise his holy name. Let all
that I am praise the Lord;
may I never forget the good
things he does for me.

PSALM 103:1–2 NLT

Remember His Love

May you determine to be done with captivity! No more rehearsing your failures or rehashing your critics' accusations.

It's time to remember God's love, His faithfulness, and His heart of affection for you. It's time to put all of your hope in the finished work of Jesus Christ.

May you put a flag in the ground this day and declare, "My hope is built on nothing less than Jesus' blood and righteousness!"

Rest in God's grace. Rely on His love. And rehearse His promises because they're true for you.

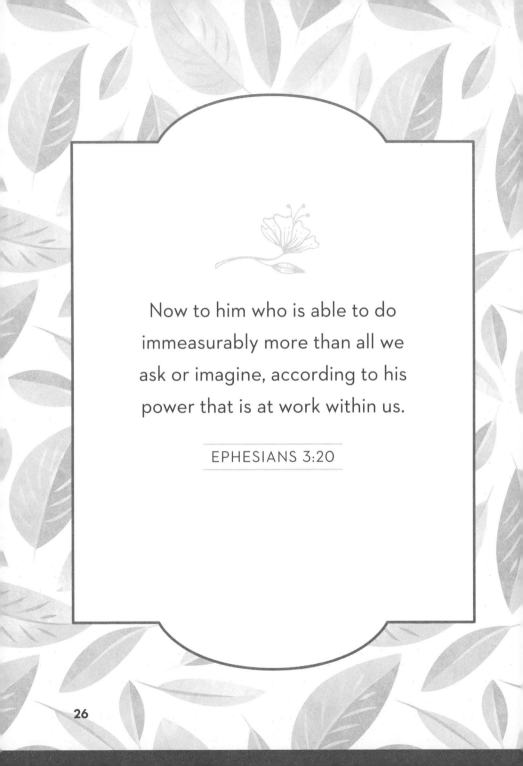

Now to him who is able to do immeasurably more than all we ask or imagine, according to his power that is at work within us.

EPHESIANS 3:20

Crazy Faith Steps

May you—above all else—see yourself as someone Jesus loves.

May His affection for you heal you in the deepest ways and inspire you like nothing else ever has.

May His saving grace and enabling power compel you to dream with Him, believe in Him, and take crazy faith steps because of Him.

May every lesser voice and every lying circumstance fall by the wayside so that all you hear is His voice in your ear saying, "This is the way, walk in it."

Nobody can save, heal, redeem, and refresh like Jesus. Walk intimately with Him today.

Whoever dwells in the shelter
of the Most High will rest in the
shadow of the Almighty.

PSALM 91:1

Pause, Rest, Reflect

May you be mindful to pause regularly and reflect on the many ways God has come through for you. This will strengthen your heart.

May you cultivate a heart that knows how to rest in God alone. This will nourish your soul.

As you look to Jesus and remember His faithfulness, your whole countenance will change and others will be reminded that there's a God in heaven very much involved in their own lives.

He intends to get us safely home. But don't wait till then to find rest in Him. Embrace a heart-at-rest kind of day.

Surely, Lord, you bless the
righteous; you surround them
with your favor as with a shield.

PSALM 5:12

Holy Confidence

May God release special favor over your life today!

May He fill you up to overflowing and give you a fresh vision for your life.

May you identify the places where the enemy has planted inferiority and insecurity and play king of the hill there! Put him under your feet and refuse to let those lies win the day.

In Christ you have NO reason to feel less than or inferior. He is more than enough for you.

Walk in God's truth and rest in His care. He loves you and He will lead you in the way you should go.

Have a blessed day today.

And we all, who with unveiled faces contemplate the Lord's glory, are being transformed into his image with ever-increasing glory, which comes from the Lord, who is the Spirit.

2 CORINTHIANS 3:18

You're Made New

May you begin to see yourself as Christ sees you.

May you understand, on a whole new level, the implications of your royal identity in Him. In Christ you are a new creation! Old things—your sins, your mistakes, your missteps—have passed away, and He's made you new, through and through.

May your unveiled face reflect His glory in ever-increasing measures as you walk intimately with Him.

You are His beloved treasure. Believe it today!

You will live in joy and peace.
The mountains and hills will burst
into song, and the trees of the
field will clap their hands!

ISAIAH 55:12 NLT

Hilarious Joy!

May the hilarious joy of the Lord burst from your heart today!

May His love sturdy your steps. May His passion fuel your steps. May His promises propel you to take faith risks.

Delight in God today. He will establish you. Rejoice in Him. He will strengthen you. Trust in Him. He will not fail you.

Wrap yourself up in His grace. You have what you need to abound in every good work. He's got you covered.

Walk with joy and gladness today.

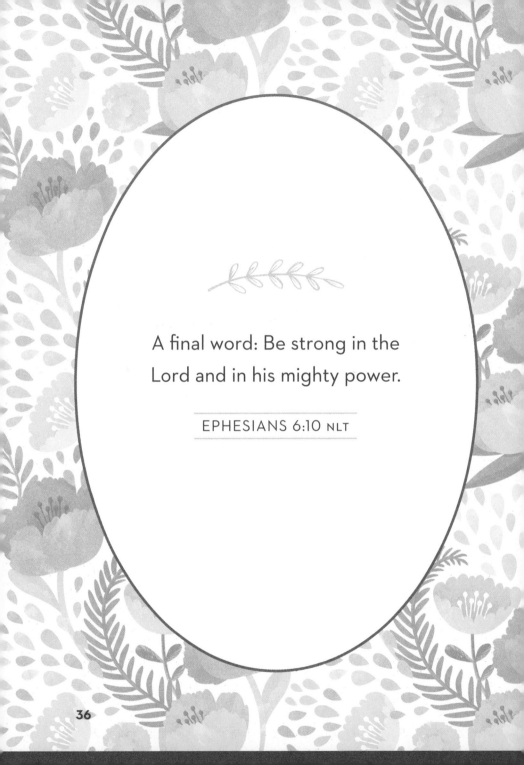

A final word: Be strong in the Lord and in his mighty power.

EPHESIANS 6:10 NLT

Remember What's True

May God fill you with grace and power this very hour!

May His love compel you to look up and remember what's true.

May crystal-clear clarity replace confusion and chaos.

And today, may you march onward with this truth alive in your soul: God is with you, He goes before you, and He has your back.

You are MORE than your circumstances. You are someone God loves and empowers to live valiantly.

Blessings on your day today.

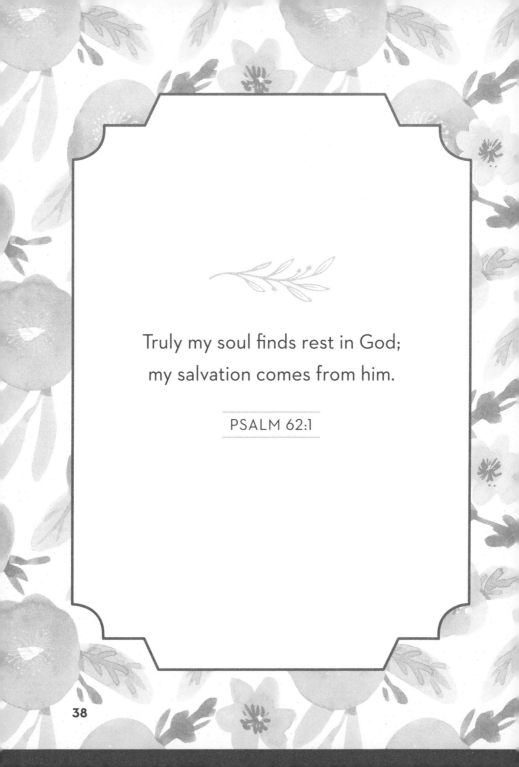

Truly my soul finds rest in God;
my salvation comes from him.

PSALM 62:1

Entrust Your Cares

May you open your hands and entrust your cares to God. Right this minute.

Know this: Jesus knows your name, has your address, and loves who you are. He will get you where you need to go. He will reach out to the ones you love. He will validate and vindicate you at the proper time.

May you see and believe that you're safest when you're at His feet, trusting Him to do what you cannot do for yourself.

May your soul find rest in Him today.

I listen carefully to what God the Lord is saying, for he speaks peace to his faithful people. But let them not return to their foolish ways.

PSALM 85:8 NLT

You Will Overcome

May you step back from the things that frustrate you and consider what God might be saying to you here.

Is He asking you to lay down your arms and entrust your soul to Him? Or is He asking you to raise your shield and stand in faith? Either way, you're not at the mercy of your circumstances. You have His mercy and He'll keep you steady and sturdy in your faith.

Don't take the bait of offense. Look up and do what Jesus tells you to do.

You will overcome!

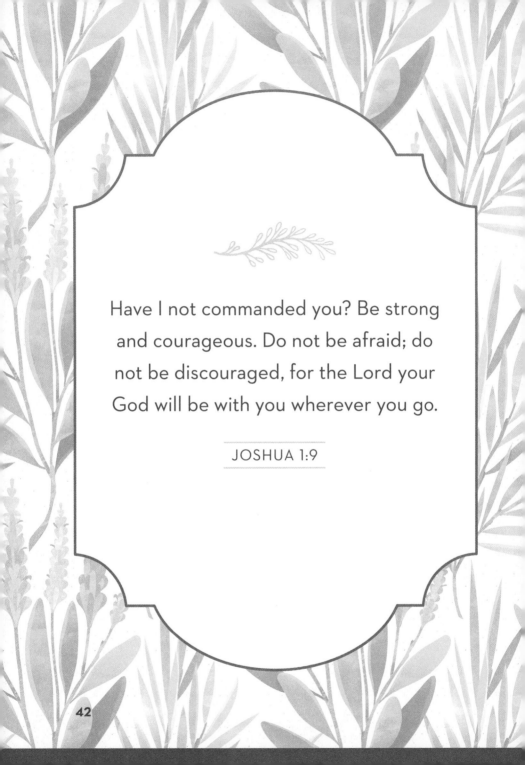

Have I not commanded you? Be strong and courageous. Do not be afraid; do not be discouraged, for the Lord your God will be with you wherever you go.

JOSHUA 1:9

Free to Be You

May God set you free from the bondage of others' opinions. May you cherish God's opinion most of all.

May you refuse to lose your joy when others don't understand you. Jesus gets you fully and loves you deeply.

You don't have to be all things to all people, because you're everything to the One who put the stars in place.

Walk confidently today. You get to be a work in progress like the rest of us.

And have a blessed and spunky day!

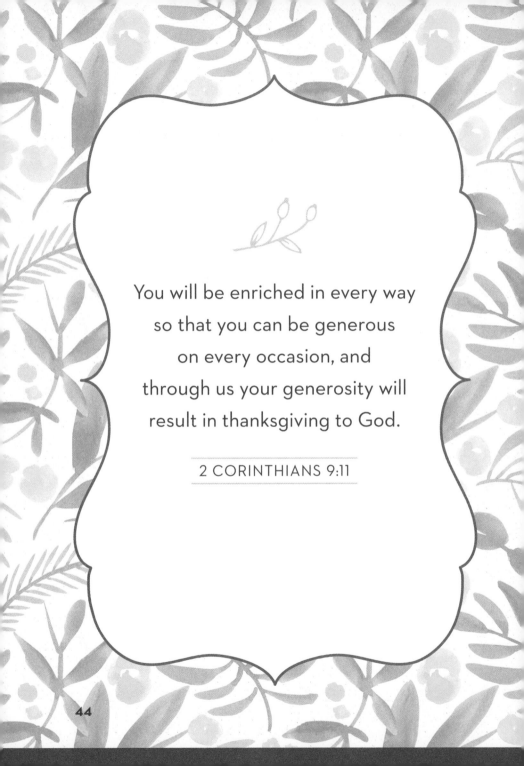

You will be enriched in every way
so that you can be generous
on every occasion, and
through us your generosity will
result in thanksgiving to God.

2 CORINTHIANS 9:11

Live Generously

May you suddenly know and believe that you are deeply loved, abundantly cared for, and profoundly called.

May you discern the heavenly resources you've yet to lay hold of.

May you begin to care more and more about the needs of others.

May you give generously as one who has an endless supply to draw from.

You are loved, called, equipped, and provided for.

Live boldly and gladly today. The Savior has you in His hand and in His heart.

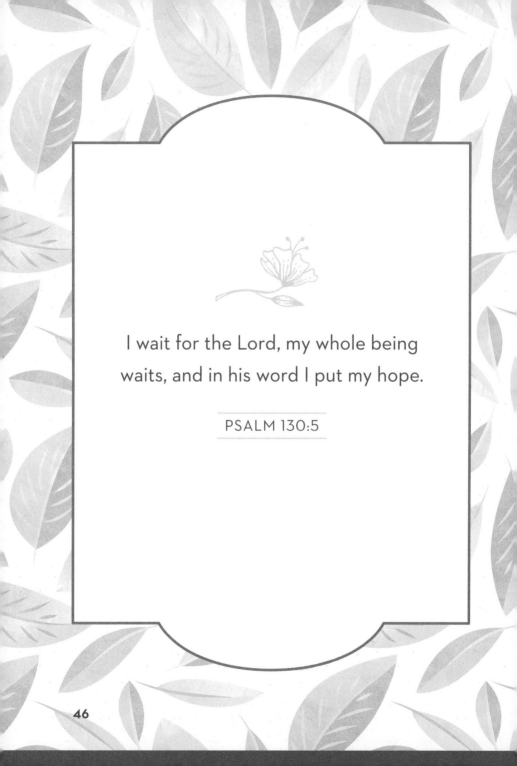

I wait for the Lord, my whole being waits, and in his word I put my hope.

PSALM 130:5

Care for Your Soul

May you become an expert at caring for your soul.

May you know when to tuck yourself under the shadow of God's wing and when to run to the battle line, knowing He will fight for you.

May you know when to rest and know when to work.

May you refuse worry and embrace faith.

May you become tenacious when it comes to the promises of God and tender when you think about His love for you.

Stay in tune with God and you'll stay in step with Him.

Have a great day.

Above all else, guard your heart, for everything you do flows from it.

PROVERBS 4:23

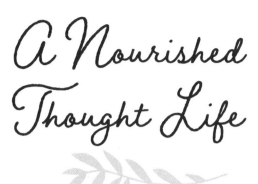

A Nourished Thought Life

May you cultivate a lifestyle that creates space for grace and growth.

May you guard against toxic thoughts, attitudes, and mindsets that only weaken you.

May you instead fill your thoughts with all that's lovely, praiseworthy, and true.

In the days ahead, may your intimate walk with Jesus inform your decisions, fuel your prayers, and magnify your love.

Guard your thoughts and it'll change your life.

Have a wise and winsome day today.

I bow before your holy Temple as I worship. I praise your name for your unfailing love and faithfulness; for your promises are backed by all the honor of your name.

PSALM 138:2 NLT

His Presence and Promises

May Jesus' presence be especially tangible to you today.

May the reality of His love sink deep into your bones.

May His faithfulness be your anchor, His promises your protection, and His presence your joy.

God is faithful and it's impossible for Him to fail you. He's made promises to you that He intends to keep. And His presence changes EVERYTHING.

Enjoy and embrace the access God has offered you today.

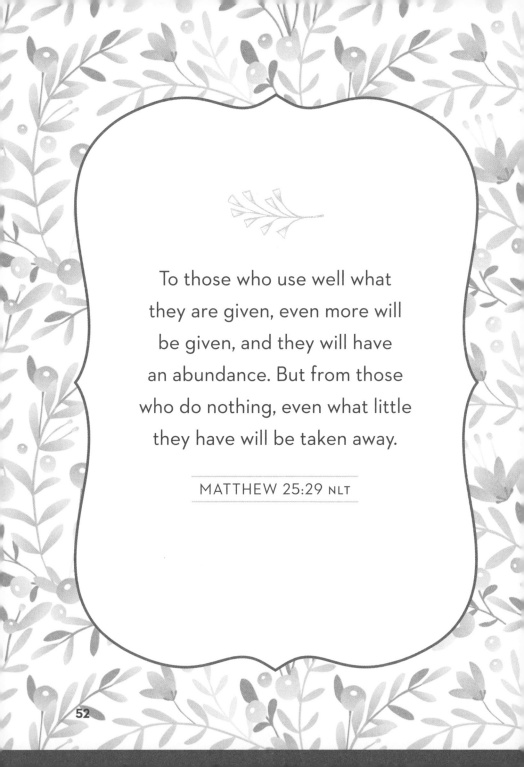

To those who use well what they are given, even more will be given, and they will have an abundance. But from those who do nothing, even what little they have will be taken away.

MATTHEW 25:29 NLT

Your Next Steps

May God bring fresh hope to your heart today!

May He make a way where there's been no way.

May He give you wisdom and peace for your next steps.

May He protect you where you're vulnerable and establish you in your calling.

May you dare to steward your time, treasures, and talents today so you are ready for what God has for you tomorrow.

Blessings on your day today.

So let's not get tired of doing what is good. At just the right time we will reap a harvest of blessing if we don't give up.

GALATIANS 6:9 NLT

Envision a Harvest

May God lift your chin, awaken your heart, and open your eyes to all you possess in Him.

May you refuse to let your disappointments define you. May you instead stand on that barren land and envision a harvest.

May you experience a revival of faith in the very place of your heartbreak! Instead of rehashing your losses, determine to rehearse His promises because they're truer than your circumstances.

Today's a good day to embrace faith, to give thanks, and to worship the One who keeps His promises.

You've got everything you need in Him.

Therefore, there is now no condemnation for those who are in Christ Jesus.

ROMANS 8:1

No Condemnation

May you divinely discern the difference between holy conviction and unholy condemnation.

May you walk wisely without walking in fear.

May you guard your heart without walling it off and shutting it down.

May you refuse the enemy's attempts to bait you into sin and captivity.

May you learn to live freely, wisely, and full of faith with each new day.

You are a royal ambassador of the Most High God. May God's richest blessings be yours today!

And I am certain that God, who began
the good work within you, will continue
his work until it is finally finished on
the day when Christ Jesus returns.

PHILIPPIANS 1:6 NLT

Ask for the Impossible

May you refuse to let your emotions dictate your perspective. You have Jesus. You have His presence. And you have His promises!

When what your eyes see is different than what your heart deeply desires, look up and pray. He invites you to walk with Him, talk with Him, and involve Him in every detail of your life.

If you're in the "not-yet" season, take time to worship God because He's God; take time to thank Him too, because He's been good.

And dare to ask for the impossible, because He's a wonder-working God.

Your story is not over yet.

For the Lord Most High is awesome.
He is the great King of all the earth.

PSALM 47:2 NLT

A Thin Veil

May the veil between heaven and earth seem especially thin.

May you sense, like never before, the presence and the power of the living God.

Jesus won the victory. He defeated death and sin. He made a public spectacle of the powers that oppose us.

Though you have troubles and trials, you serve a strong and mighty God who means what He says and does what He says He'll do.

One day there will be no more tears, no more war, no more hatred. Keep walking. Keep believing, because you're only passing through.

You're heaven bound. Live like it's true today.

A most blessed day to you!

When Jesus woke up, he rebuked the wind and said to the waves, "Silence! Be still!" Suddenly the wind stopped, and there was a great calm. Then he asked them, "Why are you afraid? Do you still have no faith?"

MARK 4:39–40 NLT

Jesus Is Near

When you can't sense what God is up to, may you trust even more His heart toward you.

When your journey is different than you would choose, may you see His invitation to make you new.

When the storm rages overhead, may you know—with everything in you—that new mercies are on the other side.

And when you're tempted to overstate your problems and understate His promises, may you step back and find your footing again.

On Christ the solid Rock you stand, all other ground is sinking sand. He is mighty to save, and He is doing a new and beautiful thing in you.

Embrace a joy-perspective this day!

Now may the Lord of peace
himself give you peace at
all times and in every way.
The Lord be with all of you.

2 THESSALONIANS 3:16

A Peaceful Soul

May God's peace mark your day in every way.

May the Lord show you places in your life where you've let your guard down, let your thoughts wander, and let your peace slip away.

May Jesus help you shore up your life once again.

May you listen more closely to His voice and turn a deaf ear to the enemy.

May you refuse thoughts and indulgences that only weaken you.

Engage in all of the things that are good for your soul. Jesus loves you and He wants what's best for you.

Have a peace-saturated day today!

Give all your worries and cares to
God, for he cares about you.

1 PETER 5:7 NLT

God of the Breakthrough

May you cast your cares on Jesus. May your load feel instantly lighter as you trust Him.

May kingdom power upstage every worry and every fear. May kingdom authority help you to rise above your circumstances instead of being crushed by them.

New days are ahead. Breakthrough days are just around the corner.

Don't give up hope. You serve the God of the breakthrough, and He is for you.

May God bless your day today!

When you ask, you must believe and not doubt, because the one who doubts is like a wave of the sea, blown and tossed by the wind.

JAMES 1:6

Seeing Beyond Obstacles

May God open your eyes to see beyond the obstacles and through the storm so you can envision His next place of promise for you.

May your doubts, worries, and fears take a backseat to faith, hope, and love. In fact, may others look up from their own storm because of how you trust God in yours.

You are mighty in battle because God is mighty in you!

Don't give up hope. Don't coddle your fears. Cling to the promises of God and walk forward in faith.

Have a brave and courageous day.

See, I am doing a new thing! Now it springs up; do you not perceive it? I am making a way in the wilderness and streams in the wasteland.

ISAIAH 43:19

A New Thing

God is doing a new thing. Can you sense it?

May you lean in and listen to that still small voice and take your next steps with faith and courage.

Soon, and very soon, you will see and know that His promises are true for you.

Strengthen yourself in the Lord today. Recite His promises and rehearse His faithfulness. God's been good, and He'll be good again.

God bless you, dear one.

For our light and momentary
troubles are achieving for
us an eternal glory that far
outweighs them all.

2 CORINTHIANS 4:17 NLT

Momentary Troubles

May the Lord Himself give you a fresh perspective on your life.

May you begin to see your troubles—tough as they are—as momentary. In fact, may you wrap your arms around the promise that those very troubles are achieving for you an eternal glory that far outweighs them all.

Jesus is deeply invested in your journey and intends to get you safely home. May He give you a glimpse of glory, a peek into the eternal significance of your life.

You matter deeply to Him.

May your spirit be renewed in His presence today.

Lord, you alone are my portion and
my cup; you make my lot secure.
The boundary lines have fallen
for me in pleasant places; surely
I have a delightful inheritance.

PSALM 16:5–6

Stay the Course

May God's grace empower you to live abundantly, to pray powerfully, and to stay the course.

May your honor for Him compel you to trust Him when your trials seem truer than His Word.

God will not fail you, will not forget about you, and will not turn away from you.

He's with you in battle, He'll help you when your heart breaks, and He'll deliver you and bless you before a watching world when the time is right.

Trust Him. You are so very dear to His heart.

Have a purposeful, powerful day.

The Lord is my light and my salvation—so why should I be afraid? The Lord is my fortress, protecting me from danger, so why should I tremble?

PSALM 27:1 NLT

Confident in Battle

May you stand strong in the face of enemy threats.

May you remain confident even when an army rises up against you.

May you put your flag in the ground and declare that if God is for you, who can stand against you? Far greater is HE who is in you, than he who is in the world.

You are God's beloved, and He will guard and guide you, shelter and provide for you, bless and establish you.

Jesus loves you, and nothing and no one can change His mind about you. He is sold on the idea of you!

May you live like you're His, because you are.

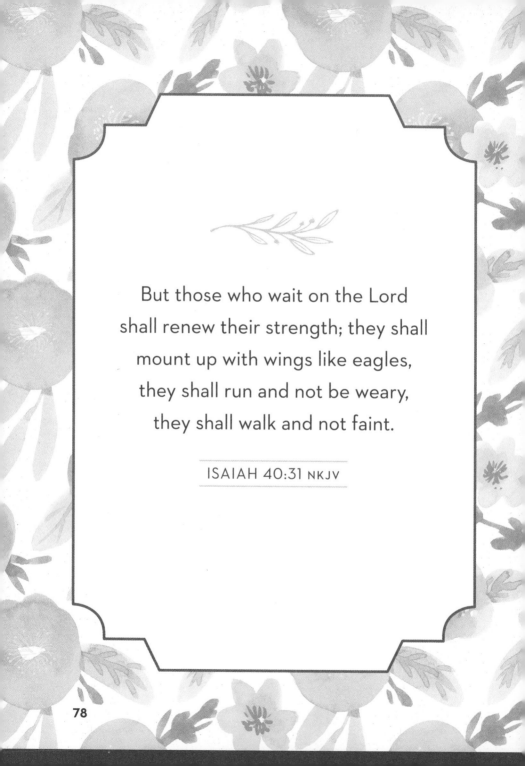

But those who wait on the Lord shall renew their strength; they shall mount up with wings like eagles, they shall run and not be weary, they shall walk and not faint.

ISAIAH 40:31 NKJV

Faith Becomes Sight

May you know in the deepest places of your soul that Jesus is working in ways you cannot see.

In due time your faith will become sight and you'll be glad that you trusted Him. Trust that He's working on your behalf.

And in the meantime, may you be generous to those in need, compassionate to those who struggle, and kind to those whom the world overlooks.

You are an ambassador of the Most High God. Trust Him with your whole life today!

He says, "Be still, and know that I am God; I will be exalted among the nations, I will be exalted in the earth."

PSALM 46:10

Holy Ground Moments

May you see the wisdom of cultivating a heart at rest, though many are caught up in the chaos of the culture.

May you notice the holy ground moments when God's movement in our midst is tangible.

May you take off your shoes, though others race right past you.

And today, may you become so assured of God's presence and His love that when others encounter you, they are compelled to look up and seek Him for themselves.

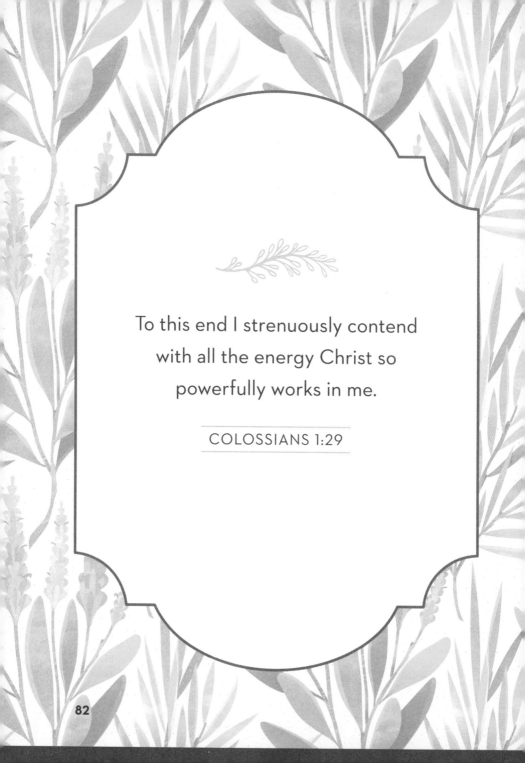

To this end I strenuously contend with all the energy Christ so powerfully works in me.

COLOSSIANS 1:29

Energy and Strength

May the Holy Spirit infuse you today with energy and strength!

May He empower you to walk courageously through your trials.

May He endear you to those in authority over you. And may He impress upon your heart those He's given you to love.

You are His ambassador, anointed for His purposes and empowered by His strength.

All of heaven is on your side. Let that amazing truth put a spring in your step today!

Give thanks to the Lord,
for he is good; his love
endures forever.

PSALM 107:1

Have Fun

May you count your blessings today out loud, one by one, in a louder voice than you'd usually use (it's hilariously fun that way).

May you remember a time you belly laughed with a friend and smile at the thought of it.

May you put on a song that makes you dance and shout and thank God for the freedoms you enjoy.

And may you stretch your arms out in faith, full of expectancy that your future days will be brighter than your past.

God is on the throne, working on your behalf, and He's always good.

So do not fear, for I am with you;
do not be dismayed, for I am
your God. I will strengthen you
and help you; I will uphold you
with my righteous right hand.

ISAIAH 41:10

Soldier On!

May new and fresh hope suddenly arise within you!

May the enemy's plan against you backfire as you grow stronger in your trials, not weaker.

May your sturdy grasp of God's promises intimidate the enemy and make him lose heart.

May you find JOY in the heat of the battle, POWER in the promises of God, and PROVISION where you've known lack.

May the things you once knew of God pale in comparison to what you know of Him now. He makes all things new. And He will come through for you.

Soldier on, mighty one! God is with you.

This is what the Lord says: "Stand at the crossroads and look; ask for the ancient paths, ask where the good way is, and walk in it, and you will find rest for your souls."

JEREMIAH 6:16

Fresh, Ancient Faith

May God grace you with a new perspective on an old situation.

May He give you fresh faith where you're feeling faint.

May He inspire new inspiration and motivation where you've lost momentum.

May Jesus bless you with new friends and may He bring new strength to your old friendships.

May you see the treasure in the old and be inspired by the new.

A blessed and beautiful day to you.

For by one sacrifice [Jesus] has
made perfect forever those
who are being made holy.

HEBREWS 10:14

Look to Jesus

When you come to the edges of yourself and you feel
the limits of your love and your generosity . . . instead of
despair, just whisper a prayer to the God who loves you.

He'll do through you what you cannot do for yourself. He
never rolls His eyes or breathes a heavy sigh when He looks
at you.

May you—in the midst of your limits—look to Jesus, who
intends to finish what He started in you.

Walk freely today, knowing you (like the rest of us)
are a work in progress. And you get to be, without the
condemnation.

Blessings on your day this day!

Rejoice always, pray continually, give thanks in all circumstances; for this is God's will for you in Christ Jesus.

1 THESSALONIANS 5:16–18

Pray Tenaciously

May you look around and notice all of the answers to prayer you enjoy because of what you prayed some time ago.

May the breakthroughs you've experienced and the open doors you've walked through compel you to pray with more fervency, specificity, and tenacity.

God loves your faith. He loves it when you pray.

He's very protective of you and won't give you something that's not good for you. He makes you wait because He's making you ready.

Keep praying. God is moving, even when you can't see it.

One day, your faith will become sight.

He gives strength to the weary and
increases the power of the weak.

ISAIAH 40:29

He'll Revive You

May God revive the areas of your life where you've lost hope and expectancy.

May you grow to believe—on a whole new level—that Jesus makes all things new. He can make something out of nothing!

May you look up right now and dare to believe once again.

God is on His throne. Jesus prays for you. And the Holy Spirit moves on faith.

Don't let go of hope. Believe that God redeems.

Rest in the reality of God's awesome love, power, and faithfulness. He'll do for you what you cannot do for yourself.

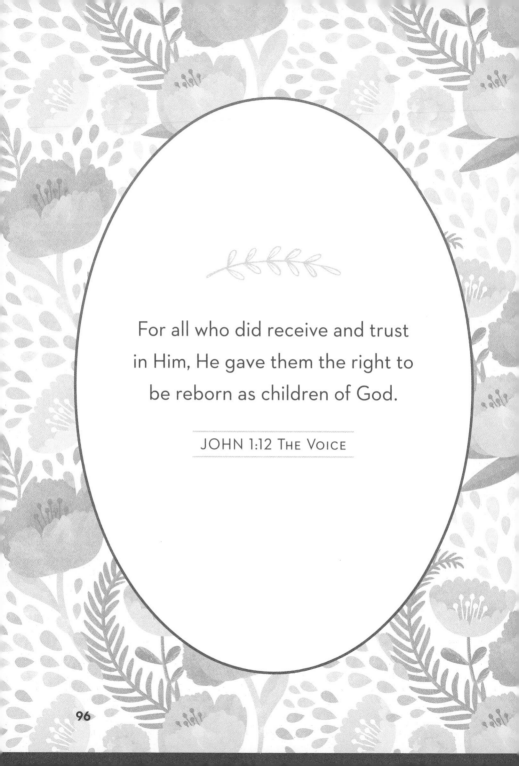

For all who did receive and trust in Him, He gave them the right to be reborn as children of God.

JOHN 1:12 THE VOICE

You're an Heir

May you walk and talk and pray and live in a manner worthy of your royal status in Christ Jesus.

May you believe with your whole heart that you are positioned right where you are, for such a time as this.

May God increase your influence, anoint your words, and appoint your everyday moments.

You are an ambassador for the Most High God. Live like it is true, because it is.

Blessings upon you this day!

From the ends of the earth I call to
you, I call as my heart grows faint; lead
me to the rock that is higher than I.

PSALM 61:2

Keep Perspective

May you ponder what God is saying to you in this place of not-yets and what-ifs. Do you hear His whisper to be still and to trust Him?

May you dream big dreams in the face of your fears.

May you courageously hold your ground when you'd rather run and hide.

And may you entrust your heart's desires to a God who is very much involved, very much in control, and very much invested in your life.

Remember who you are. Remember Whose you are.

Keep perspective. Lay hold of faith. Take the next step.

May the God of hope fill you with all joy and peace as you trust in him, so that you may overflow with hope by the power of the Holy Spirit.

ROMANS 15:13

Enjoy the Joy

May a new sense of expectancy and hope rise up within you.

May you look up from the things that frustrate you and find new reason to dance and sing.

Joy is yours for the taking. Celebrate God's goodness in THIS place!

May your history with God compel you to enjoy Him today and trust Him with your future. He loves you passionately and powerfully every single day.

You are blessed. Be strong. Enjoy the joy!

Trust God from the bottom of your heart; don't try to figure out everything on your own. Listen for God's voice in everything you do, everywhere you go; he's the one who will keep you on track.

PROVERBS 3:5–6 THE MESSAGE

Listen for Him

May you be so sensitive to God's voice that you rest when He says rest and run when He says run. He knows what's best for you and He'll get you where you need to go.

When it comes to your pace and your choices, people will always have their opinions about you, but God offers His power to you.

He's the one who knows your frame, your steps, and your story. Trust Him and do what He says.

Though there are giants in the land, you have God on your side. Be courageous.

He's got you.

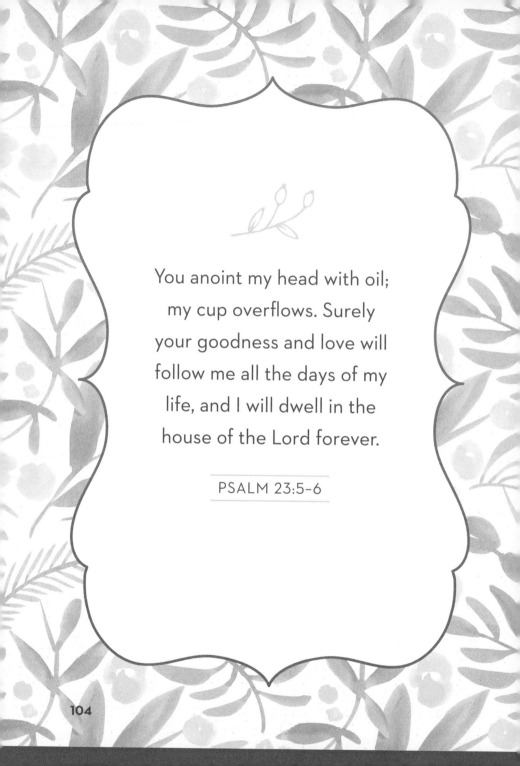

You anoint my head with oil;
my cup overflows. Surely
your goodness and love will
follow me all the days of my
life, and I will dwell in the
house of the Lord forever.

PSALM 23:5–6

Fresh Anointing

May the Lord Himself pour out a fresh anointing on your life today.

May you suddenly have a heightened discernment about where to walk, what to say, and how to pray.

May the Lord fill you afresh with new insights from His Word.

May your taste for things that weaken you be replaced by a hunger for that which strengthens you.

May God open your eyes to the importance of your life and your calling.

And may you find strength and courage with every faith-filled step you take.

You are mighty in God.

Have a great day today!

May you experience the love of Christ, though it is too great to understand fully. Then you will be made complete with all the fullness of life and power that comes from God.

EPHESIANS 3:19 NLT

Jesus Loves You

No matter what you're going through, may you know in the depths of your soul that you are loved.

Your identity is completely secure. It's not up for grabs or changeable with popular opinion. Jesus loves how He made you!

Seasons come and seasons go, but God's love for you never changes. It is abundant, profound, and amazingly real, right here, right now.

Walk like you're loved, because you are, beyond your wildest dreams.

Have a beautiful day!

How priceless is your unfailing love, O God! People take refuge in the shadow of your wings. They feast on the abundance of your house; you give them drink from your river of delights. For with you is the fountain of life; in your light we see light.

PSALM 36:7–9

He Sings Over You

May you cup your ear toward heaven and listen to Jesus' song over you, for it's healing, redemptive, and life-giving.

When you are tempted toward melancholy or to listen to contrary voices, may God's truth and His song lift your chin and fill your heart.

Even your battles can serve you well if you trust God's heart for you in the midst of them.

Remember this: God is with you and for you and it's impossible for Him to fail you!

Lean in to Jesus today. He's got you.

The Lord directs the steps of the godly. He delights in every detail of their lives. Though they stumble, they will never fall, for the Lord holds them by the hand.

PSALM 37:23–24 NLT

He'll Make a Way

May the Lord Himself establish you in His highest and best purposes for you.

May He open doors, move mountains, and bring provision in the very near future.

May He confirm your faith steps and energize your prayers. He is mighty, He is good, and He cares about every detail of your life.

May you obey Him and do what He says. He's making a way where there is no way.

He loves you truly and deeply. Trust Him today.

You make your saving help my shield, and your right hand sustains me; your help has made me great.

PSALM 18:35

Jesus, Your Shepherd

May you cherish this truth: The Lord is your very dear and precious Shepherd. In Him, you have everything you need.

He'll lead you to still waters and sacred spaces to restore your soul.

He'll lead you in paths of righteousness for His name's sake.

Even when you walk through the deepest valley, He'll be right there with you, close beside you.

He'll correct and direct, guide and provide, and He'll never forsake you.

His goodness and mercy will chase after you all the days of your life.

God invites you to dwell in the house of the Lord all the days of your life.

And this is my prayer: that your love may abound more and more in knowledge and depth of insight, so that you may be able to discern what is best and may be pure and blameless for the day of Christ.

PHILIPPIANS 1:9–10

Increase Daily

May you abound in love more and more.

May you increase daily in all wisdom, knowledge, and depth of insight.

May you understand the times and know what to do.

May your passion for the things of God grow exponentially.

May you lose heart for your unappointed commitments so you'll be ready for your kingdom assignment when He calls you to it.

You're not made for this place. You're only passing through.

Walk full of faith, hope, and love today.

He will cover you with his feathers. He will shelter you with his wings. His faithful promises are your armor and protection.

PSALM 91:4 NLT

Marvel Today

May you marvel today that Jesus came to earth to save you, so that you, as a redeemed soul, can live FOREVER with Him.

Pause today and consider the miracle of salvation, the wonder of God's love, and the power of His truth to set us free.

Though you have troubles, you will triumph because Jesus says so.

Keep walking. Keep praying. Keep asking. Keep believing.

You're not alone. You're not under your circumstances.

You are under His wing and He will keep you close to His heart.

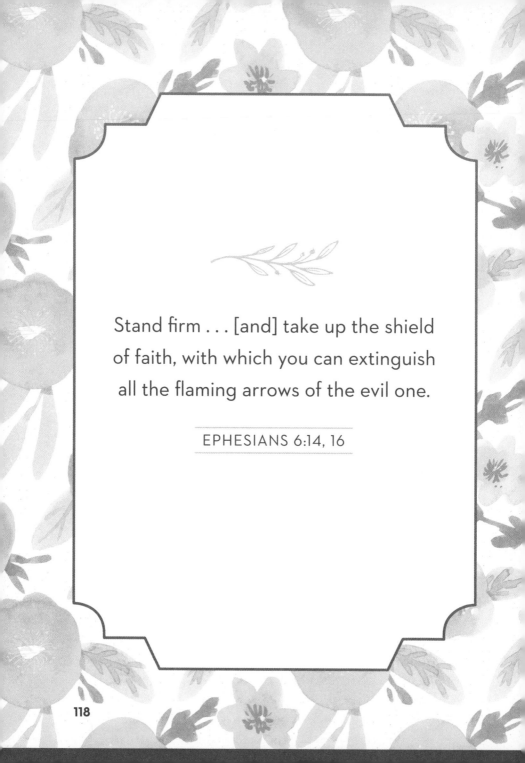

Stand firm . . . [and] take up the shield of faith, with which you can extinguish all the flaming arrows of the evil one.

EPHESIANS 6:14, 16

Raise Your Shield

May you raise your shield of faith, draw a line in the sand, and tell that enemy of your soul, "No more! You will steal from me no longer!"

Refuse to be bullied by your fears.

Don't put up with the enemy's taunts and threats. Put him under your feet where he belongs.

Remember the authority you have in Christ.

Pray God's Word with all the passion in your soul.

Raise your shield and lift your voice.

God has made you an overcomer!

For we are God's masterpiece.
He has created us anew in Christ
Jesus, so we can do the good things
he planned for us long ago.

EPHESIANS 2:10 NLT

You're a Masterpiece

As you walk intimately with Jesus, may faith feel as natural to you as breathing in and breathing out.

Pause throughout the day to look at the sky, to notice a child, or to help someone in need, and remember that you belong to Creator God. He made you for a purpose and placed you on this earth for such a time as this.

Breathe in His promises, breathe out His Word, and remember His goodness. You are His masterpiece.

Walk with joyful, humble, bold confidence today.

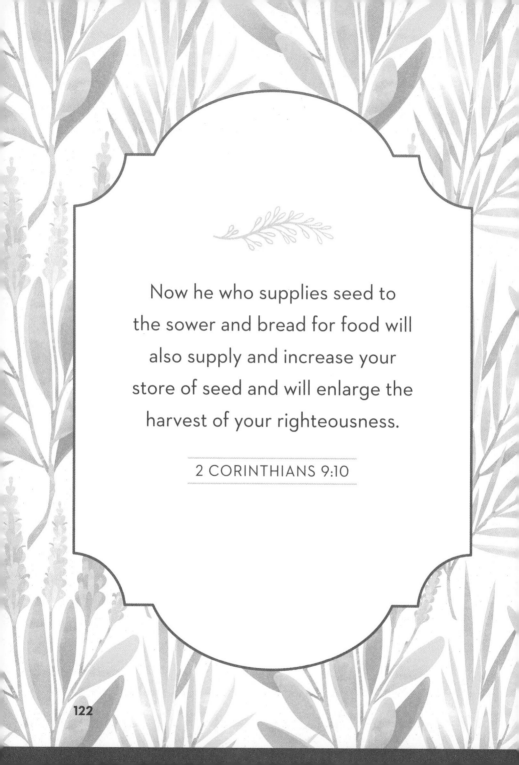

Now he who supplies seed to the sower and bread for food will also supply and increase your store of seed and will enlarge the harvest of your righteousness.

2 CORINTHIANS 9:10

The Wonder of Small

May you begin to cherish the wonder of small things: small seeds, baby steps, subtle shifts in perspective.

When God is about to do a new thing, He starts small and speaks to those who are listening. Are you listening?

Don't underestimate the power of your kindness, obedience, offerings, and prayers. Do small things like they're big things.

Open your hand and trust Him to make something out of practically nothing. He's a wonder-working God and loves to work through you.

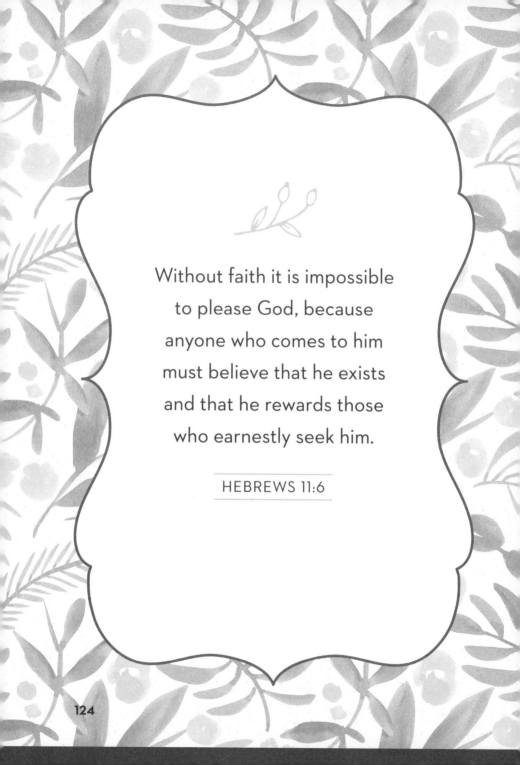

Without faith it is impossible
to please God, because
anyone who comes to him
must believe that he exists
and that he rewards those
who earnestly seek him.

HEBREWS 11:6

A Faith Adventure

May you follow Jesus to the edges of your comfort zone to get a glimpse of where He's taking you.

May you put everything on the table and give Him permission to rearrange your life.

May you dare to unclench your fists, look up, and breathe a prayer of thanks right in the midst of this uncertain time, knowing that He's far kinder than you can fathom and far greater than you ever imagined.

Can you sense Jesus' invitation to join Him on this adventure of faith? Will you trust Him?

Your security is found in Jesus!

I remain confident of this: I will see the goodness of the Lord in the land of the living. Wait for the Lord; be strong and take heart and wait for the Lord.

PSALM 27:13-14

You'll See His Goodness

When your faith seeds are in the ground and the harvest is yet to come, may you use the time in between to care for your soul and to know Jesus more.

Are you weary? Give priority to rest.

Are you disillusioned? Take some time in God's presence and let Him renew your perspective.

Do you feel beat up by life? Draw near to Jesus so He can restore you.

Don't forget who you are in this season of life. You are loved, treasured, called, and appointed.

God has not lost your address. He knows where you live. And at just the right time, He will break through.

Be courageous today!

Let us stop going over the same old ground again and again, always teaching those first lessons about Christ. Let us go on instead to other things and become mature in our understanding, as strong Christians ought to be.

HEBREWS 6:1 TLB

Detoxify Your Soul

May the Holy Spirit detoxify your soul!

May He show you what needs to go so He can strengthen you for the road ahead.

May you get a glimpse of His plan for you, just enough to inspire you to make the necessary changes and take hold of His promises.

May you be willing to do something different so you'll be ready and equipped for this next place of promise.

He's got a new chapter ahead for you. You are so precious and important to Him!

Blessings on your day today.

"For I know the plans I have for you,"
declares the Lord, "plans to prosper
you and not to harm you, plans to
give you hope and a future."

JEREMIAH 29:11

A Window of Heaven

May you pause today and look above your disappointments and frustrations.

Do you see Jesus in this place? He is with you, for you, and will surely sustain you.

He intends to strengthen your faith, sturdy your frame, and stir up a fresh passion for His name. He is stronger than your fears, greater than your hurts, and deeper than your insecurities.

May Jesus open a window of heaven and give you a glimpse of who you are because you are His. He sings over you, and in due time He will deliver you.

May a renewed perspective be yours today!

Do not conform to the pattern of
this world, but be transformed
by the renewing of your mind.
Then you will be able to test and
approve what God's will is—his
good, pleasing and perfect will.

ROMANS 12:2

A Wise, Discerning Day

May you be highly discerning in the days ahead!

May you know when God is asking you to shore up your faith and stand strong and when He's inviting you to hide yourself under the shadow of His wing.

May you quickly discern the enemy's schemes and stay clear of his traps.

In spite of your mistakes, missteps, and misunderstandings, may you never doubt your worth and your value.

God will show Himself strong in your weakness, faithful in your fears, and merciful where you fall short.

Walk wisely with Him today. There's a best place—a best path—for your feet.

The Lord is my strength and shield. I trust him with all my heart. He helps me, and my heart is filled with joy. I burst out in songs of thanksgiving.

PSALM 28:7 NLT

You're Amazing in Him

May you choose joy today, because in Christ Jesus you are stronger than you know!

May you engage your faith today, because God moves when you pray in faith.

May you walk confidently today, because Jesus paid a high price for your soul. You matter deeply to Him.

May you show compassion today, because you've received such compassion from God Himself.

You are wrapped up in God's promises, strengthened by His care, and called by His divine will.

Everything you need you already have in Him.

The Lord replied, "My Presence will go with you, and I will give you rest."

EXODUS 33:14

A Replenishing Lifestyle

May you cultivate a lifestyle that allows for times of replenishing rest, powerful prayer, and thoughtful consideration to what God is saying to you in this season.

God is with you. His activity surrounds you.

Jesus is near, yet the culture races on as if He doesn't exist. But He lives! And His promises are true for you.

Open your hands and let Him fill them. He gives good gifts to His children, and you are someone He treasures.

The godly may trip seven times,
but they will get up again.

PROVERBS 24:16 NLT

Get Back Up Again

When life knocks you down, may you get back up again because God is mighty in you!

When your rogue emotions turn you upside down, may you find your footing again because your Rock is Christ.

When the clouds block the sun and your perspective dims, may God Himself break through with a fresh reminder of His promises.

May the changeable things in your life take a backseat to the unchangeable, never-ending love and faithfulness of God.

He has given you a sturdy place to stand.

You go before me and follow
me. You place your hand of
blessing on my head. Such
knowledge is too wonderful for me,
too great for me to understand!

PSALM 139:5–6 NLT

New Beginnings

May God give you glimpses of the new beginnings He has for you.

May you stay in step with Him and trust Him in the meantime.

May God give you joyful contentment in the place He has you now.

May you faithfully steward your current assignment as you wait for God to move you.

May you see the treasure of trusting the timing of your dreams to God. He is with you, and He cannot, will not fail you.

Sing for joy today and trust Him fully with your tomorrows.

So if the Son sets you free,
you will be free indeed.

JOHN 8:36

Your Story Matters

May you tune out the noise of the world and lean in and listen to what Jesus has to say to you today. Your story matters to Him. He is with you on this journey.

He offers peace that passes understanding and strength in the midst of your weakness.

His Spirit in you defies the gravity of the past you'd rather forget.

You are forgiven and free. You have nothing to prove and all of eternity to live for.

Live free today. Embrace His life within you today. And stay in step with Him today.

Nothing can ever separate you from Jesus' love.

"For in him we live and move and have our being." As some of your own poets have said, "We are his offspring."

ACTS 17:28

Tastes and Preferences

May you trade your time-wasters for things that nourish and strengthen your soul.

May you turn your back on influences that diminish and distract you from the abundant life God offers you.

May you give more time to that which is life-giving and soul-sustaining.

May you carefully guard your tastes and preferences so you don't lose your taste for the things of God.

Nothing on this earth and no one else can satisfy our souls' deepest longings like Jesus can.

You are made for Him. Find your life in Him today.

Take delight in the Lord, and he will give you the desires of your heart.

PSALM 37:4

Something More, Something Deeper

May you sense God's invitation to believe Him for something more, something greater, something deeper.

When unbelief overwhelms you, may you refuse despair and instead respond in prayer, "Lord, awaken fresh faith in me!"

He holds out His hand and bids you to walk on the water with Him, to trust Him with what breaks your heart, and to believe that He is the one who put some of those dreams in your heart.

Look up and trust Him today. He is faithful to His Word, and He has made specific promises to you.

Return to your rest, my soul, for
the Lord has been good to you.

PSALM 116:7

You Are Blessed

May you start and end your day with thoughts of God's goodness.

May you right here, right now, lift your hands and praise Jesus for the many blessings you enjoy!

He came to earth to save you. He promised He'd never leave you.

And you have water to drink, clothes to wear, food to eat, and people to love.

You have the promise of heaven and a purpose to fulfill.

You have the Father, Son, and the Holy Spirit.

You're richer than you know and more blessed than you can fathom.

Live like you're loved and blessed today because you really, truly are!

You will show me the way of
life, granting me the joy of your
presence and the pleasures
of living with you forever.

PSALM 16:11 NLT

God's Awesome Presence

May your precious heart for Jesus upstage your fears about today and your worries about tomorrow.

May His awesome presence so transform you that the opinions of others lose their hold on you.

May God's very real love for you spill out in the way you love others.

May the guidance and direction of the Holy Spirit take you where you never thought you'd go and help you accomplish what you never dreamed possible.

God will do great things in and through you if you trust Him. So trust Him!

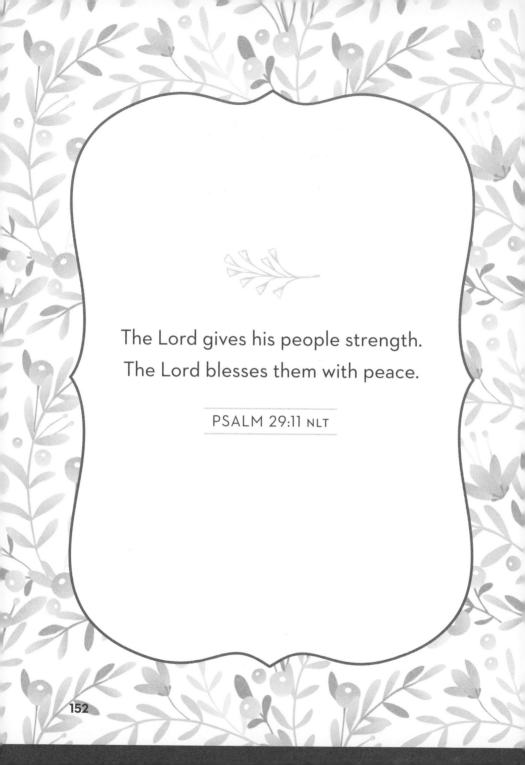

The Lord gives his people strength.
The Lord blesses them with peace.

PSALM 29:11 NLT

He Speaks Life

May Jesus lift your chin today and speak life into your weary soul.

May you remember afresh how very much He loves you.

May your bumps and bruises be healed in His presence.

May you shake off today's frustrations and tomorrow's worries.

Rest in the reality of His divine involvement in your life. Jesus is more than enough for you.

Listen for His life-giving invitation to you. And choose joy as you walk through your day today.

Humble yourselves before the Lord,
and he will lift you up in honor.

JAMES 4:10 NLT

Humble and Hopeful

May you be humble when it comes to your strengths and profoundly hopeful amidst your weaknesses.

The One who put the stars in their place knows all about you, and He sings over you!

You're not who you once were, you're not even what you do. You are someone He loves and enjoys.

Open your hands and surrender your heart as an offering to Him.

He'll renew and restore you, strengthen and encourage you.

He'll never leave and never forget about you.

He'll get you safely home.

Lean in close and trust His heart for you this day.

For the Lord God is our sun and our shield. He gives us grace and glory. The Lord will withhold no good thing from those who do what is right.

PSALM 84:11 NLT

In the Storm

As you survey the parts of your life that break your heart or that don't make sense right now, may you dare to stand strong and consider afresh what God's resurrection power can do in you!

Only those who've walked through the valley of the shadow will truly grasp the power of redemption on the other side.

Jesus withholds NO good thing from those who walk intimately with Him.

He's not the reason you suffer; He's with you in the storm.

He is your Shelter, Deliverer, and Strong Tower.

He's your Redeemer, Savior, and Friend.

He's your Prince of Peace and Sure Defender.

Trust Jesus with your whole heart, and see what Love will do.

I will heal their waywardness
and love them freely.

HOSEA 14:4

For Your Loved Ones

May God answer your accumulative prayers for the ones you love.

May He open their eyes, heal their wounds, and restore their perspective.

May He cut off every person and circumstance that sends a lying message to them, and may He make their crooked ways straight.

May He restore the weary, heal the broken, and bring the prodigals home.

And may you wait with joyful expectancy, because God moves when you pray.

Rest in the promise that God loves your loved ones far more passionately than you do!

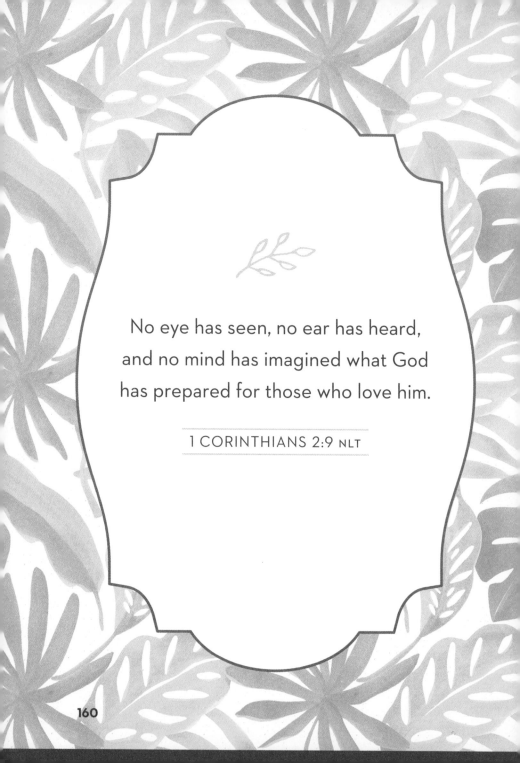

No eye has seen, no ear has heard,
and no mind has imagined what God
has prepared for those who love him.

1 CORINTHIANS 2:9 NLT

Scoot Closer

May you, amidst your everyday life, dare to scoot a little closer to Jesus and listen to what He has to say to you.

He loves you. He cherishes you. He has hopes for you. He wants to heal you, restore you, and renew you.

His truth will set you free. His power will part the waters. His love will heal your soul. His heart for you will make you whole.

Listen for His voice today; it's gentle, powerful, redemptive, and life-giving. Oh, how He loves you!

May you believe who you can be because of Him.

Have a blessed and beautiful day.

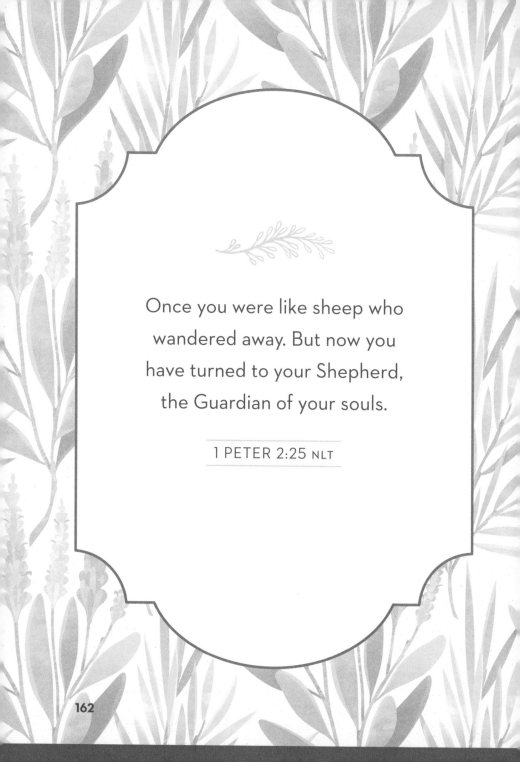

Once you were like sheep who wandered away. But now you have turned to your Shepherd, the Guardian of your souls.

1 PETER 2:25 NLT

Have a Brave Day

May you be a tender, teachable Christ-follower and respond to God's invitation to make you more like Him.

Whenever He calls you up, it means He's getting ready to call you out to a new place, a new assignment, and a new land of promise.

Refuse the enemy's taunts.

Respond to the Guardian of your soul. He loves you and intends to use you greatly.

Have a brave day.

Anyone who belongs to
Christ has become a new
person. The old life is gone;
a new life has begun!

2 CORINTHIANS 5:17 NLT

Startling Clarity

May God give you startling clarity about His plans for you.

May you find utter joy in His presence because He fully enjoys you!

When He sets the plow a little deeper in the soil of your character, may you refuse despair. Instead, may you know that in Christ there is never any condemnation, only an invitation.

God corrects and redirects because He's about to do a new thing. So lean in. Listen with your heart.

Do what He says. Respond in faith. And trust that God's will for you is your best-case scenario.

Devote yourselves to prayer,
being watchful and thankful.

COLOSSIANS 4:2

Powerful in Prayer

May you become a powerful, praying saint!

May you pray prayers that make your knees buckle and your heart tremble.

Jesus intends to solve some of the world's problems through you. This is no time for cowering in fear. This is a time to rise up in faith!

Trust God's Word. Believe His promises. Do what He says. And in due time, you'll see the waters part, the mountains move, and the answers you've been waiting for.

You are mighty in God.

Walk full of faith today.

He will wipe every tear from their eyes, and there will be no more death or sorrow or crying or pain. All these things are gone forever.

REVELATION 21:4 NLT

Lift Your Eyes

May the reality of heaven be more tangible than your temporary troubles.

May the promise of God's provision compel you to give generously and live with expectancy.

May you see the blessing in your battles. Even in hardship, Jesus meets us, refines us, and empowers us to change the world.

May you refuse to get tangled up in your regrets from yesterday, your frustrations today, and your fears about tomorrow.

Lift your eyes and look to Jesus.

Have a blessed, magnificent, eternity-minded day!

So then, just as you received Christ Jesus as Lord, continue to live your lives in him, rooted and built up in him, strengthened in the faith as you were taught, and overflowing with thankfulness.

COLOSSIANS 2:6–7

A Grounded Sense of Hope

May God do such a deep healing work in your soul that you're able to look at your disappointments and heartbreaks with a grounded sense of hope.

May your emotions rest on God's unchanging love for you.

Your Rock is Christ, and He is immovable. Stand on Him. Stand strong because of Him.

And know this: One day He'll make your righteousness shine like the dawn and will reveal to the world that you belong to Him!

Find your sturdy place in Him today.

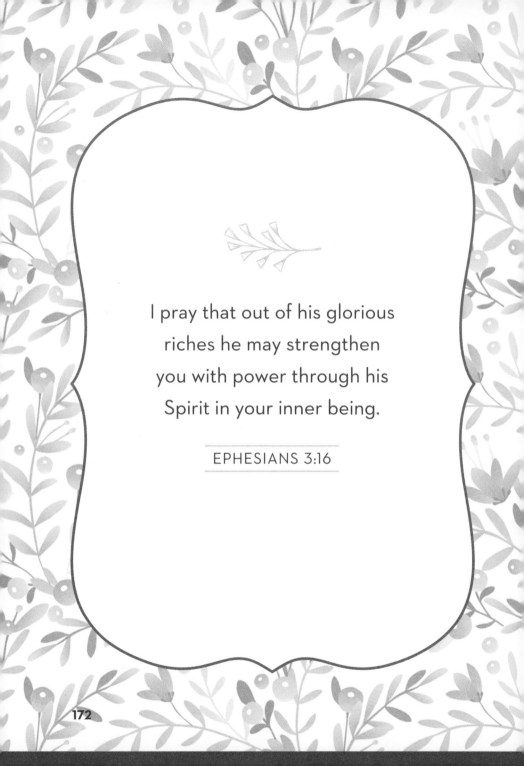

I pray that out of his glorious
riches he may strengthen
you with power through his
Spirit in your inner being.

EPHESIANS 3:16

This Very Moment

May God, this very moment, lift your heavy load and breathe fresh life into your weary sails.

May He give you relief from your pain, rest from your fears, and refreshment in your perspective.

Sometimes we just need to pause, open our hands, and give back to God the things we're holding so tight. May Jesus help you!

May the Holy Spirit infuse you with power and inspire you to trust Him more fully.

May your mind, body, soul, and spirit experience an awakening as you trust Him with your cares and take Him at His word.

You long to enthrone truth throughout
my being; in unseen places deep
within me, You show me wisdom.

PSALM 51:6 THE VOICE

Be Unoffendable

May you be quick to identify and let go of any lies you pick up along the way today.

May you shake off any offenses that you're tempted to cling to.

May you instead wrap yourself up in the complete love and affection of Christ. May you forgive yourself and forgive others.

May you believe that God's promises are more powerful than your blunders.

Embrace God's redemptive plan for your life with hope and expectancy. You are truly, deeply loved.

You make your saving help my
shield, and your right hand sustains
me; your help has made me great.

PSALM 18:35

Emotional Rest

May your emotions find rest in God alone while you wait for Him to answer your prayers.

May you dare to sing a new song even when sighing feels easier to do.

May you slow down and sit down for a while, just for the sake of rest and reflection.

And when you get up again, may you find new resolve to stand firmly on God's promises and to walk forward in faith.

If you take one humble, bold step at a time, you'll eventually put your toes on your promised land.

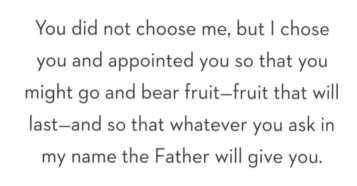

You did not choose me, but I chose you and appointed you so that you might go and bear fruit—fruit that will last—and so that whatever you ask in my name the Father will give you.

JOHN 15:16

The Abiding Life

May you let go of what you can't control and lay hold of what God has promised you.

In these days of chaos and evil, may you stand up and be counted, and may you bow low and pray powerfully.

May you look up when you need perspective and look around you for who needs your help.

May you actually accomplish with less effort because you've learned the secret of the abiding life.

Be much with Jesus. He'll do great things through you.

The thief does not come except to steal, and to kill, and to destroy. I have come that they may have life, and that they may have it more abundantly.

JOHN 10:10 NKJV

Holy Conviction

May you refuse condemnation for the ways you fail and fall short.

May you instead, with holy conviction and passion, embrace God's grace to live like Jesus.

May you shake off your regrets and grab a firm hold of God's promise to forgive, restore, and renew your story.

May others' opinions no longer tie you up in knots, because God's opinion continually sets you free!

May you determine with all your heart to live the abundant, powerful, forgiven life Jesus has offered you.

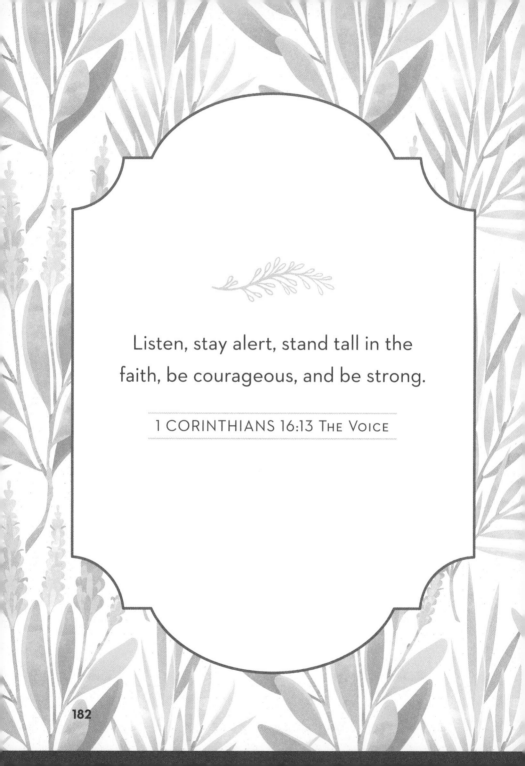

Listen, stay alert, stand tall in the faith, be courageous, and be strong.

1 CORINTHIANS 16:13 THE VOICE

Pray Audaciously, Obey Immediately

May Jesus Himself open your eyes to His activity on the earth today.

May God give you insight into others' stories so you will know what to say and when to say it.

Instead of looking too long at the enemy's wicked schemes, remember this: Whenever the devil makes a move, God already has a plan and His purposes WILL prevail.

Pray audaciously. Obey immediately. God has you on the earth today for a reason. May He find faith in you.

Blessings on your day today.

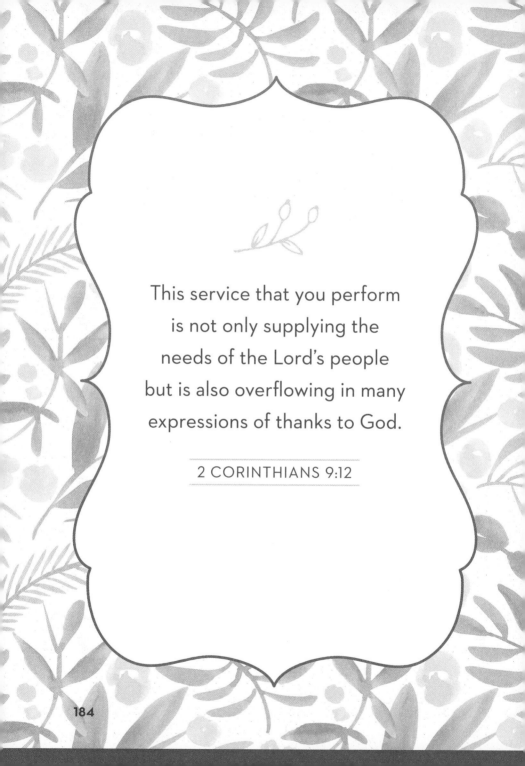

This service that you perform
is not only supplying the
needs of the Lord's people
but is also overflowing in many
expressions of thanks to God.

2 CORINTHIANS 9:12

No More Striving

May you refuse to strive for appearance's sake because you are established for Jesus' name's sake.

You are loved, treasured, appointed, and anointed.

You are free to climb mountain heights with joy and free to stumble and fall without the condemnation.

Jesus holds you and will lead you safely home.

Know His love. Trust His heart. Be yourself. And do only what He asks you to do.

Have a heart-at-rest sort of day today. He's got you!

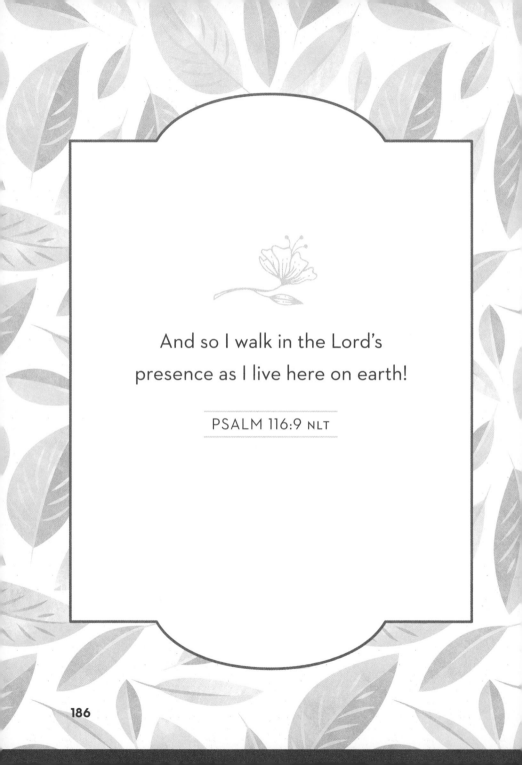

And so I walk in the Lord's presence as I live here on earth!

PSALM 116:9 NLT

Your Highest Aim

May Jesus breathe fresh life into your soul and fresh courage to face your fears.

May you sense His hands on your face, and may you hear Him speak words of truth, affection, and redemption over you.

May your awareness of His love make every lesser affection fade away.

He is your highest aim, your most lofty goal, your greatest prize. And you have Him!

May you live every single day with the grace and mercy He provides. He's with you.

I am leaving you with a gift—peace of mind and heart. And the peace I give is a gift the world cannot give. So don't be troubled or afraid.

JOHN 14:27 NLT

More of Jesus

May Jesus increase His territory through you!

May you allow Him more access to your soul, more influence in your life, and more voice in your choices.

And when you come to the edges of yourself and you're hemmed in by your own humanity, don't despair—rejoice. There's more of Jesus for you!

The enemy of your soul wants you focused on your disappointments and limitations. The Savior of your soul wants you to look up and believe Him for great things.

Don't let your heart be troubled. May Jesus answer your prayers and profoundly love the world through you.

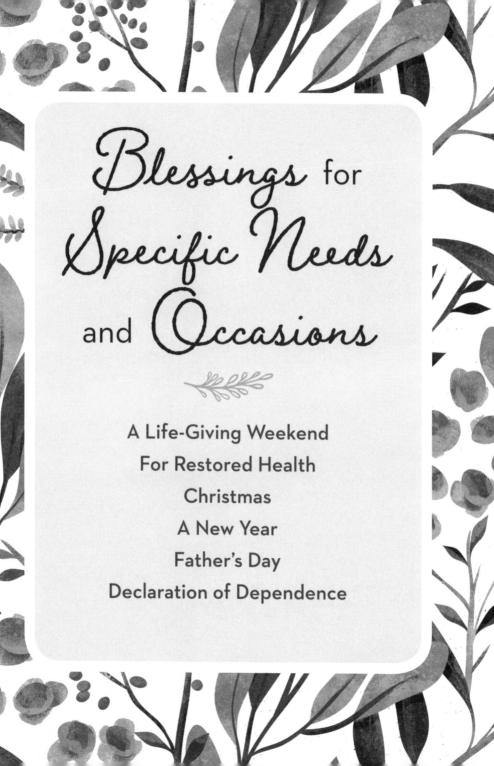

Blessings for Specific Needs and Occasions

A Life-Giving Weekend

For Restored Health

Christmas

A New Year

Father's Day

Declaration of Dependence

And whatever you do, whether in word or deed, do it all in the name of the Lord Jesus, giving thanks to God the Father through him.

COLOSSIANS 3:17

A Life-Giving Weekend

May you slow down and make time for rest and reflection.

May you pick up that book you've wanted to read, listen to music that nourishes your soul, and try that recipe that sounds good to you.

May you take yourself less seriously and take God more seriously.

May you laugh with abandon, pray with power, and love the way Christ has loved you.

May this for you be a sacred, life-giving weekend.

Bless you!

Everyone tried to touch him,
because healing power went out
from him, and he healed everyone.

LUKE 6:19 NLT

For Restored Health

May God's perfect love swallow up every single fear and anxious thought.

May Jesus renew your perspective in a way that brings you peace and assurance.

In Jesus' name, may sickness and disease bow down at the feet of Jesus and flee from your body this very moment.

May your loved ones find their strength in Christ alone.

May God do for you what you cannot do for yourself.

And may your every moment be filled with grace and peace, healing and rest, perspective and power, in Jesus' name. Amen.

But the angel reassured them. "Don't be afraid!" he said. "I bring you good news that will bring great joy to all people. The Savior—yes, the Messiah, the Lord—has been born today in Bethlehem, the city of David."

LUKE 2:10-11 NLT

Christmas

May your expectations of what the holidays should look like fall by the wayside.

May you believe that God cares about your loved ones and will work in ways you cannot fathom.

May you see glimpses of glory that surprise and bless you.

May He do a miracle in your heart so that you can receive all He wants to impart to you. He's a miracle-working God.

Jesus came to earth to seek and save the lost. May you be found in Him this Christmas season.

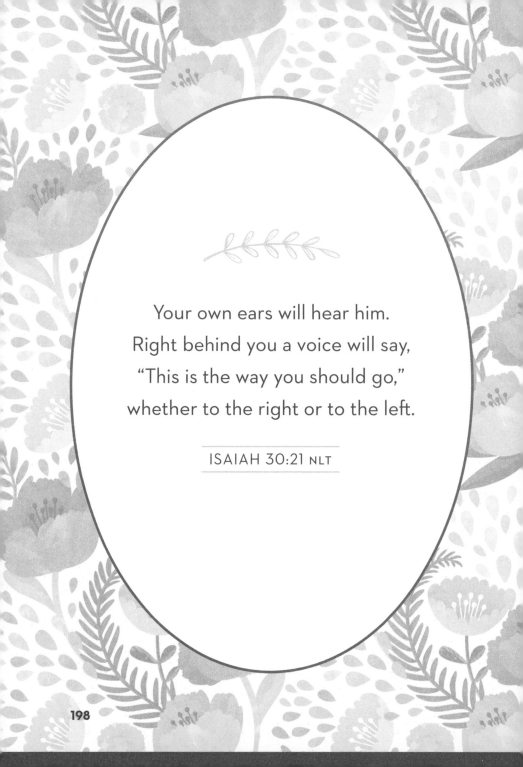

Your own ears will hear him.
Right behind you a voice will say,
"This is the way you should go,"
whether to the right or to the left.

ISAIAH 30:21 NLT

A New Year

In this new year, may you grow to love the sound of God's voice in your ear!

May you develop a hunger and a thirst for all God has for you.

You are a gifted, treasured, loved person, and you're called to impact the world in a way that only you can.

May the love of Christ constrain you and compel you in the days ahead.

May He open your eyes to the new territory awaiting you.

Even if my father and mother abandon me, the Lord will hold me close.

PSALM 27:10 NLT

Father's Day

Whether you had a father who loved you or a father who was absent, know this: You have a Father in heaven who is very much taken with you.

He loves you, cares for you, and wants you to know how much He treasures you.

He cares about your hurts, cares about your hopes, and intends to get you safely home.

May Jesus heal your wounds, refresh your heart, and inspire a new expectancy.

May you take Him at His word and see what's possible when you believe.

We serve a good God who loves us, and He's an amazingly present Father.

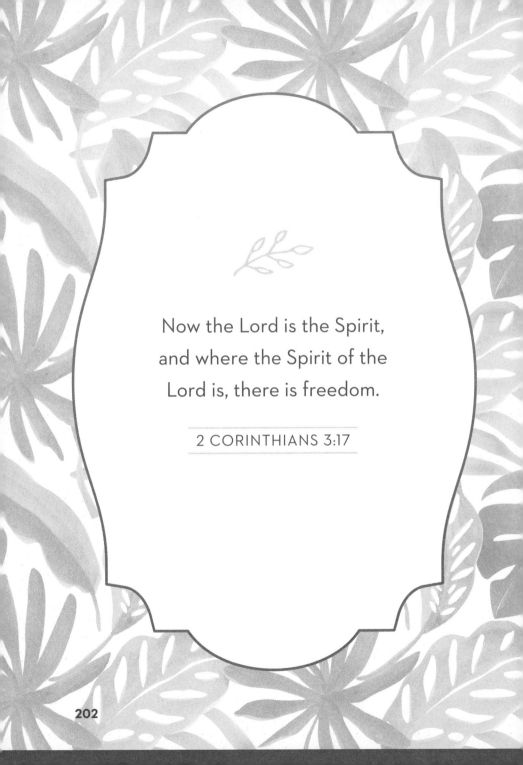

Now the Lord is the Spirit,
and where the Spirit of the
Lord is, there is freedom.

2 CORINTHIANS 3:17

Declaration of Dependence

May your heart burst with gratitude for the freedoms you enjoy.

May you take a fresh look at the territory God has entrusted to you and offer it back to Him.

May you dwell in the land and feed on His faithfulness.

And may this be your declaration of dependence: "It is for FREEDOM that Christ has set me free. I will live with boldness, courage, and conviction. I will love freely, give generously, and pray passionately. And, I will entrust my whole soul and story to God because I belong to Him. Thank you, Jesus, You've set me free!"

Special thanks to:

My friends at Bethany House Publishers
You are amazing kingdom people.

My literary agent, Steve Laube
You gave my message wings.

My assistant, Lisa Irwin
You serve in the most excellent way.

My intercessors
You are mighty in God.
Thanks for standing in the gap for me.

My friends and family
We are in this together.

My Savior, Jesus
Because You are
the greatest blessing of all.

Susie Larson is a popular media host, author, and national speaker. For eight years she hosted her own daily talk show, *Live the Promise with Susie Larson.* A veteran of the fitness field, Susie has also served as a media voice for Moody Radio and was the former cohost for Focus on the Family's daily live talk show, *Everyday Relationships with Dr. Greg Smalley.* Her passion is to see women and men everywhere strengthened in their faith and mobilized to live out their high calling in Jesus Christ.

Susie has twice been voted a top-ten finalist for the John C. Maxwell Tranformational Leadership Award. This award recognizes people who go beyond themselves to make a positive impact in the lives of others. Her books include *Fully Alive, Your Powerful Prayers, Your Beautiful Purpose, Your Sacred Yes, Growing Grateful Kids, The Uncommon Woman, Blessings for the Evening,* and *Blessings for the Morning.*

Susie and her husband, Kevin, live near Minneapolis, Minnesota, and have three adult sons, three beautiful daughters-in-law, one amazing grandson, and one adorable pit bull. For more information, visit susielarson.com.

May the Lord bless you
and protect you.
May the Lord smile on you
and be gracious to you.
May the Lord show you his favor
and give you his peace.

NUMBERS 6:24–26 NLT

More Wisdom and Inspiration from Susie!

Visit susielarson.com for more information.

In this eye-opening book, Susie Larson shows how intertwined our emotional, spiritual, and physical health is. For true healing to occur, it must happen holistically—mind, body, and spirit. Providing a fresh vision of what a flourishing life is, Susie shares practical, biblical ways to walk the path of healing and wholeness in every area of life.

Fully Alive

Start and end each day with an uplifting reminder of God's promises, love, and purpose for you. Instead of focusing on your worries and concerns, replace them with these daily doses of encouragement rooted in God's Word.

Blessings for the Morning and Evening

BETHANYHOUSE

Stay up to date on your favorite books and authors with our free e-newsletters. Sign up today at bethanyhouse.com.

facebook.com/BHPnonfiction

@bethany_house_nonfiction

@bethany_house

More Wisdom and Inspiration from Susie!

Visit susielarson.com for more information.

Through personal stories and biblical insights, Susie Larson shares the secrets to effective prayer in this warm and wise book. You'll be amazed at what your prayers can do when you combine reverence, expectation, and a tenacious hold on God's promises. Discover how to pray specifically and persistently with faith and joy!

Your Powerful Prayers

It's so easy to give away our time to things un-appointed by God. In this practical and liberating book, Susie invites you to say no to overcommitment and yes to the life of joy, passion, and significance God has for you.

Your Sacred Yes

◆ BETHANYHOUSE